Author's Note

This book reflects my personal journey through mental health challenges, including a diagnosis of Borderline Personality Disorder (Borderline Personality Disorder (BPD)).

All stories are shared for healing, awareness, and advocacy, not as justification or defense.

Names and identifying details have been changed where appropriate.

Nothing in this book should be interpreted as a reflection of my current professional conduct or capacity. I am committed to safe, ethical leadership and ongoing mental health management.

The views and opinions expressed in this book are those of the author and do not reflect the official policy or position of any agency, employer, or organization.

A Journey Through Borderline Personality Disorder-Healing and Resilience

By N. Alleyne

Copyright © 2025 N. Alleyne

All rights reserved.

No part of this book may be reproduced, distributed, or transmitted in any form or by any means, including photocopying, recording, or other electronic or mechanical methods, without the prior written permission of the author, except in the case of brief quotations embodied in reviews or articles.

ISBN: 9798218770181

Readers Introduction:

This book invites you into a deeply personal journey through mental health, self-discovery, and healing. At the heart of these stories is my experience living with Borderline Personality Disorder (BPD); a diagnosis that helped me make sense of years of emotional chaos, silent battles, and misunderstood behaviors.

What you'll read here isn't about excuses or explanations. It's about truth. These pages are offered as a form of healing, awareness, and advocacy for those who live with BPD, and for those who love them. My hope is that by telling my story, others will feel less alone in theirs.

Names And Identifying Details Have Been Changed Where Appropriate.

Nothing In This Book Should Be Interpreted As A Reflection Of My Current Professional Conduct or Capacity. I Am Committed To Safe, Ethical Leadership And Ongoing Mental Health Management.

The Views And Opinions Expressed In This Book Are Those Of The Author And Do Not Reflect The Official Policy Or Position Of Any Agency, Employer, Or Organization.

Table Of Contents

Note to Readers:

The following chapters include raw reflections on moments from my unhealed past. These stories are not shared for shock or sympathy. They are shared as a testament to how deep the pain once ran and how far I've come. I no longer live in that space. I share these truths to honor the journey from breakdown to breakthrough.

Chapter 1: When Rage Was My First Language................pg.11
Chapter 2: Motherhood Broke Me, Then Built Me..........pg. 18
Chapter 3: Pretty, Perfect, And Falling Apart.................pg. 24
Chapter 4: What They Don't Tell You About Healing ....pg. 29
Chapter 5: Boundaries Saved My Life ....pg. 33
Chapter 6: I Am Not My Diagnosis ....pg. 39
Chapter 7: Healing Is Not Linear ....pg. 43
Chapter 8: Keeping Your Shit Together....................…..pg. 47
Chapter 9: How To Love Me (And People Like Me).......pg. 51
Chapter 10: When The Rage Took Over ....pg. 57
Final Chapter: The Girl Outside the Door..................pg. 64

Trigger Warning / Content Advisory

Content Warning:
This book includes descriptions of self-harm, suicidal ideation, childhood trauma, and mental illness. Please read with care. If you find yourself feeling overwhelmed, it's okay to pause. You deserve safety, even in your healing.

Resources for Mental Health & BPD Support

- National Suicide & Crisis Lifeline: Dial 988
- Therapy for Black Girls: www.therapyforblackgirls.com
- National Alliance on Mental Illness (NAMI): nami.org
- DBT Self-Help Tools: www.dbtselfhelp.com
- Angie Cares Advocacy: @ac_parentadvocacy on Instagram

This book is a reflection of personal lived experiences and is not intended to replace professional mental health advice, diagnosis, or treatment. While it discusses symptoms related to Borderline Personality Disorder and other mental health conditions, it should not be considered a clinical resource. If you or someone you know is struggling, please reach out to a licensed mental health provider.

Dedication

For my father, **Ben,** who gave me stability and pride, even when life felt uncertain.

For my sons, **Kamryn** and **Kaeden,** my greatest teachers and my deepest love.

For **Dr. Lethermon,** whose wisdom helped me peel back the layers and keep walking toward healing.

For my bff/sister, **Chavon,** my built-in best friend and therapist, I owe you at least a million dollars in unpaid co-payments.

For **William**, thank you for loving me gently, offering disclaimers when I needed grace, and never asking me to be less than my whole self.

For **Gina,** thank you for seeing the educator in me before I ever did, for guiding me with both wisdom and heart, and for becoming the godmother I never knew I needed.

For my cousin, **Megnon** , the first person I trusted enough to see me fully, your presence at my lowest gave me safety I didn't know I needed.

For my **Family**, near and far, whose presence, whether soft or stormy, shaped this story in more ways than one.

And for **Lorenzo,** my sweet emotional support dog, who never judged me for crying in the middle of the day or talking to myself like I had a full audience.

You each held pieces of me when I didn't know how to hold myself. Thank you for loving me through it.

For My Mother

Though our time together was marked by pain, distance, and silence, I carry you with me.
I don't know exactly why, but I thank you.
For giving me life.
For the pieces of you I see in myself.
For the strength I found in your absence.

Your story shaped mine.
And in some strange, sacred way… I am still loving you through it.

Rest in peace.

Preface

This book began on impulse, written during a wave of emotional overwhelm, which I now recognize as a hallmark of Borderline Personality Disorder. What started as a release quickly became a reckoning. The more I wrote, the more I began to understand myself without shame, and to recognize that my story, like so many others deserved to be told.

I wrote this for those living with BPD, especially the ones who mask it so well that no one sees the battle. I wrote it for Black women who are often denied the space to break down, be vulnerable, or heal publicly. I wrote it for the daughter still waiting at the door, the mother trying to get it right, the professional holding it all together, the human just trying to survive and those that love them.

When I started, I was still healing through the eyes of my younger self. Today, I write as a woman learning to extend grace to all the versions of me that carried me here.

I feared judgment; still do. But I'm not sorry for telling the truth. Our truth matters.

If you find yourself in these pages, I hope you feel seen. I hope you feel held. And I hope you know you are not alone.

—N. Alleyne, M.Ed., M.A.
Educator, Advocate, Survivor, Storyteller

Author's Note

To my father, Ben White…

This is not your story. But I could not tell mine without you in it. You gave me stability when life was chaos, and your presence grounded me even when the world didn't make sense.

You'll see parts of me in these pages that you may not have known. Please know nothing here is meant to hurt. It's here to *heal*.

Thank you for loving me the way you always have; completely.

Love always,
Lil Darlin'

Chapter 1: When Rage Was My First Language

Shit Gets Real

> *This Chapter Cracks Open The Hard Shell Of Survival Mode. It Explores How Rage Becomes A First Language When Vulnerability Feels Unsafe. For Some Of Us, Crying Had To Be Relearned. What Starts As Silence Eventually Becomes A Scream For Help—And Then, With Healing, A Soft Exhale.*

Before I ever understood softness, I spoke rage.
Before I ever learned to cry, I learned to fight.
Before I ever felt safe, I was already angry.

Growing up, rage wasn't just an emotion, it was the culture. It was the rhythm in my house. The way my daddy moved through the world was loud, sharp, and furious. From the moment he got home to the moment he left again; he was a cussin' and a fussin'. That fire soaked into my skin before I even knew what emotions were supposed to feel like.

I was the baby of the family. My two older brothers were six and seven years older than me: quiet, observant, more reserved.

But me? I was wrecking shit.

I fought at school. I fought at church. I fought with my cousins. I tried to fight my older brother. If you looked at me too long, I was ready. And if I couldn't fight *you*, I'd fight myself.

I used to slap my own thighs until they stung, hold my breath until I felt dizzy, cut myself with eyebrow archers, burn my skin with erasers. My body became the battlefield when no one else was around.

🧠 BPD Insight: *When Rage Feels Safer Than Tears*

Self-harm is not always a cry for attention, it's often a desperate attempt to feel in control.
For many living with Borderline Personality Disorder, pain becomes a language when emotions are too big and words feel unsafe. When you've been taught to suppress your feelings, your body can become the only place left to express them.

▶ **If you've ever hurt yourself just to feel something or to make the feelings stop, you're not alone. There is help. There is healing.**

I remember my daddy saying it plain one day when I was six: "Something different about that one."
He wasn't wrong. I stayed ready.

But the rage wasn't always loud. Sometimes it was calculated. Cold. I knew how to cut with my words. I remember catching my little cousin alone and saying some off-the-wall stuff, real evil little girl shit just to get in her head. I didn't want her over at my house. And if she came? I'd make sure she was scared.

I wore a mask in front of adults, but behind closed doors, I was chaos with a smile.

There was no talking back in my house, so I found other ways.
I'd go to my room and unleash.

Snap a CD. Destroy a Walkman. Slam something into the wall just to watch it break.
If I couldn't break *things*, I'd try to disappear.

I'd ball myself up under a blanket, sweat it out like a storm trapped in flesh, and cry until I passed out.

I did that for years.

Even in high school, I'd sit between the bed and the wall, covered up, locked away.
I wasn't just angry. I was overwhelmed.
I was misunderstood.
I was drowning in emotions I had no name for.

But what the world saw? A fighter.
What my daddy saw? A mouthy girl who needed to calm down.
What I felt? Rage.

As a child, I acted out what I saw around me, repeating the language and behaviors I was exposed to. I didn't have the words for trauma, but I tried to process it through control, through reenactment, through mimicry. I wasn't trying to hurt anyone. I just needed somewhere safe to release the chaos inside me. Looking back, I know now that what I was doing wasn't about cruelty. It was survival.

That was the only outlet I had.
I couldn't cry.
I couldn't talk.
But I could *unleash*.

💬 BPD Insight: *When Unmet Needs Turn Into Unseen Wounds*

When emotional needs go unmet, they often show up in unexpected ways.
For children, especially those living with early trauma; play becomes a mirror. The games they play, the stories they act out,

the silence they keep… it all reflects the chaos they can't name. The violence we internalize becomes the violence we mimic, even quietly, even alone.

▶ **If you ever acted out what you couldn't speak, your pain wasn't invisible, it was just misunderstood.**

By middle school, I was labeled "weird." But weird is just code for "we don't understand you."
My body was constantly clenched, my forehead tight with tension. I rarely smiled. I stayed on edge like a war might break out at any moment.

I didn't know how to use my words.
Anger was the only emotion I could count on.
And I was good at it.

Then came therapy.

I didn't really learn how to cry until I was 36.
Not fake crying. Not the angry cry. But that deep, soft cry, the one that says *I finally feel safe enough to let this out*.

That happened in therapy.
After I finally submitted to it, *really* submitted, I found something I didn't even know I was missing: the freedom to cry.

Now I cry all the time.
I cry when I'm happy.
When I'm sad.
When I'm proud of myself.
Sometimes just because I need to.

It's a release.
A healing.
A luxury I didn't know I deserved.

My boys have seen that shift in me too.

They've seen their hard mama grow soft.
They've seen me apologize.
They've seen me choose silence over slapping.
They've seen me break but in a way that builds.

One of the most pivotal moments of my healing journey came during a family therapy session.
I invited my closest relatives, people who had witnessed or contributed to my pain.
I wanted them to *see* what I had been carrying.

My daddy, who used to shut down every tear with, "Don't start that crying shit," sat across from me.
He had done that to my brothers.
He had done that to me.
He didn't realize the damage until I told him.

But in that session, he listened.
He heard me.
And something in him shifted.

Now we have a system.
A safe word: **"Daddy, JUST PRAY."**

When I say that, he knows to stop everything.
No jokes.
No solutions.
Just presence.

He prays.
I cry.
And together; we heal.

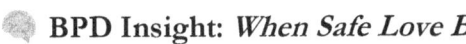 BPD Insight: *When Safe Love Becomes Medicine*

A trusted relationship where you don't have to explain your pain just express it can change everything.
Many people with Borderline Personality Disorder carry deep attachment wounds, trauma from not being seen, soothed, or safe. Healing doesn't just happen in solitude; it happens through connection. Repair begins when someone shows up consistently, listens with empathy, and stays.

➤ **If you've ever felt unlovable, know this: safe love rewires what trauma taught you.**

Rage was my first language.
But now, I'm fluent in other emotions too.

Sadness.
Joy.
Stillness.
Peace.

And when I cry now, it's not weakness.
It's proof that I survived.

Reflection Prompts: *When Rage Was My First Language*

- What emotion did you learn first as a child?
- How did the adults around you express anger or avoid it?
- When did you first realize your anger was trying to protect you?

Chapter 2: Motherhood Broke Me, Then Built Me

Crying Over Spilled Silence

> *Motherhood Came Before Healing. This Chapter Tells The Truth About Trying To Be A Good Mother While Still Mothering Yourself. It's Raw, Unfiltered, And Speaks To The Quiet Breakdowns Behind The Beautiful Pictures. And That Breakthrough On The Couch? That's The Beginning Of The Rebuild.*

I became a mama before I ever figured out how to mother myself.

I was 23 years old. A junior in college. In love. Pregnant with twins. Engaged. Living in a house I couldn't afford, trying to wear every title at once: student, wife, mama, grown.

It looked good on the outside.
The world clapped. "Look at her doing it all."
But inside, I was crumbling.

Nobody told me what postpartum depression was.
I just thought I was tired.
Sad.
Overwhelmed.
Failing.

I hadn't healed from my childhood, but now I had babies watching me, needing me, loving me. And I was still trying to figure out how to love myself.

Some days, I was an amazing mom.
We went everywhere together; me and those car seats and that big double stroller. I was active. I was present. I was *on it*.

But don't let me have a bad day.
Don't let me fall out with a man or argue with a friend.

Boom.
Everyone could get it.

I was unpredictable, the kind of mama who would light up a room… or light somebody up, depending on my mood.

After the divorce, I was a single mama with two four-year-olds and a brand new teaching career. I enrolled them in a good school, got us a new place with a tennis court and a 9-foot pool, and still found time to travel. We were good… until I wasn't.

The shift came when I called one of my sons' names and he flinched.

That broke me.

Because all I did was holler. I wasn't even physically abusive but I realized my voice alone was enough to scare them. That's when I saw it: I had become my father.

I was the "not my baby" mama too.
Let somebody mess with one of mine and I was up at that school ready to act a fool.
I was their protector, *as long as I was in a good mood.*

If they forgot to tell me they needed a poster board at 9 PM the night before it was due?
All hell could break loose.

I wasn't just reacting, I was *repeating*.
Repeating the same chaos I grew up in.
And I was handing it down.

I remember the moment it clicked.

One of the twins cleared his entire desk at school in a rage.
He was in third grade.
He was eight.
And he was me.

How could I fix the behaviors I had passed down… if I hadn't even fixed them in myself?

There were nights I would pray in the bathroom.
Put the boys to bed, close the door, and fall apart.

"Lord, help me.
I don't know what I'm doing.
I can't get it together.
My kids are copying my worst parts.
And I don't know how to stop it."

And when the prayer didn't feel like enough, I'd cry.
Sometimes I'd cut.
Then I'd cry again.
Mad that I still felt stuck.

I'd tell the boys, "Ya mama a little crazy," and they'd laugh it off but they didn't know.
They didn't know how hard I was working to keep the mask from slipping all the way off.

From the outside, we looked like a success story.

They were clean, respectful, well-mannered.
They made good grades; of course they did, I was a teacher.
We smiled for pictures.
They had haircuts, coordinated outfits.
It looked like I had it together.

But let one of them get mad?

Whew.
The generational curses were loud.
Hollering.
Fighting.
Disrespect.
Right in front of the house.
They were becoming what I had never intended.

And I knew it was because of me.

You can't raise Black boys who can't regulate.
The world won't give them the grace I failed to teach them.

Their daddy?
Calm. Steady. Loving.

But they took after their mama.

So I decided to get serious about healing.
Not for Instagram.
Not for church.
But because I could see the damage forming right in front of me.

And I was the blueprint they were following.

I tried everything.

Therapy.
Church.
Baptizing the boys.
Reading self-help.
Masking my pain behind achievement.

I bought a house when they were eight.
On paper, I was winning.

But inside?
I was unraveling.

Whether divine intervention, fate, or sheer chance, I was given another chance at life. And I chose to take it. That was the moment everything began to change.

That moment forced everything into focus.

I couldn't keep living like that.
And I *damn sure* couldn't raise them like that.

So I went back to therapy, this time ready to stop hiding.
Fully clothed from head to toe, covering my scars, but open in a way I had never been.

I rocked back and forth on that couch and said the truest thing I've ever said:

"Something is wrong with me.
I can't get a hold of it.
I don't know what it is.
It's affecting my life, my children…
and I just can't live like this anymore."

That was the day everything changed.
That was the beginning of *me*.

 BPD Insight: *When You're Mothering Through the Mess*

If you've ever looked at your child and felt guilty for not being more healed…
If you've ever built a whole life while your inner world was falling

apart...
If you've ever whispered, "Something is wrong with me," while wiping tears in silence.

▶ **You are not a bad mother. You are a human being trying to break generational patterns without a blueprint. That's not failure. That's courage.**

I wrote this for you.

I was the mama who looked strong in public but was unraveling behind closed doors.
I didn't want kids.
I didn't feel soft.
I didn't know how to mother without fear or love without control.
But I chose to stay.
I chose to try again.
I chose to heal, for them and for me.

You are not a bad mother.
You are a human being.
And if motherhood broke you, it can also rebuild you.

Healing didn't start when I looked better. It started when I finally told the truth.

Reflection Prompt: *Motherhood Broke Me, Then Built Me*

- How did becoming a caregiver change your identity?
- What part of yourself did you lose while trying to "hold it together"?
- What have your children (or your inner child) taught you about healing?

Chapter 3: Pretty, Perfect, And Falling Apart

The Mask I Wore

> *This Chapter Unveils The Quiet Unraveling That Happens Behind The Applause. When Perfection Becomes A Performance, And Healing Requires Removing The Mask—No Matter Who's Watching. This One Is For The Strong Ones Who Secretly Break Down In Silence.*

There was a time when I tried so hard to appear put together that I was literally falling apart inside.

I was the pretty one. The smart one. The one everyone counted on. But I was dying quietly.

Depression doesn't always look like sadness.
Sometimes it looks like achievement.
Performance.
Overcommitment.
Perfectionism.

I didn't just wear the mask.
I *was* the mask.

I remember when I started slipping.
Not in a dramatic, movie-scene kind of way.
But in a slow, silent unraveling.

My hair wasn't done.
The house stayed messy.
I was clocking in at work, cooking dinner, and tucking the boys in at night, but I wasn't there. Not really.
I'd drop dinner on the table, take something to knock me out, and go to sleep.

For two years, they raised themselves.
I was a shell.

It got worse.

Harder to eat. Harder to sleep.
Harder to care about anything at all.

One of the twins, barely in middle school, looked at the pile of fast food and said,
"Ma, stop buying food."

That stopped me in my tracks.
They noticed.
And I realized I had dropped 30 pounds without even knowing it.
I couldn't feel joy. I couldn't function. And the darkness started creeping back in.

The suicidal thoughts weren't loud at first.
Just whispers.

I used to fantasize about all of us going to sleep in the garage and waking up in heaven.
That's how bad it got when they were little.

But now?
They were twelve.
They *wouldn't* just go to sleep.
They'd have to live through it.
And I couldn't do that to them.

So I did something radical.

I filed FMLA.
Swiped my last credit card.
And checked myself into therapy.

Not no baby session either.
I needed *deep* therapy.
Saltwater under the bed. Ancestors on the altar. Jesus on speed dial.

But no matter how much help I sought, the self-hate still crept in.
I beat myself up for needing help in the first place.
That's what perfectionism does.

 BPD Insight: *When Pain Is Louder Than Prayer*

For people with BPD, emotional pain can be so intense that regular support doesn't touch it.
"Just pray about it" isn't enough. Sometimes the suffering is so loud, so unrelenting, that self-harm feels like the only way to quiet it. It's not about attention, it's about survival.

▶ If you've ever felt ashamed for needing more than encouragement and faith to survive the day; you're not weak. You're in pain. And pain deserves care, not judgment.

One 30-minute session wasn't going to fix me.
If I hadn't had kids, I probably would've checked into a hospital.

Because the pain?
It was unbearable.
I'd cry at work. Wipe my eyes and teach a class.
Put on a smile while falling apart inside.
But the mask… it was slipping.

People could tell.
Even my daddy looked at me sideways, his little darling, struggling to breathe.

I had always hidden it well.
Until I couldn't anymore.

And when I relapsed?
I relapsed *hard*.

It only takes a second to go too far.
I looked like I had been attacked by a bear.
Deep cuts. Raw skin. Tears I couldn't control.

My boys saw it.
They knew what it meant.

"Oh shit... she really is crazy."

And that broke me all over again.

Chapter Reflection: If This Felt Familiar...

If You'Ve Ever Looked Okay On The Outside While Dying On The Inside...
If You'Ve Ever Smiled Through Tears And Whispered, "I'M Fine"...
If You'Ve Ever Feared The People You Love Seeing The Real You—
Then You'Re Not Alone.

This Chapter Is For Every Woman Who'S Had To Keep Going With Bleeding Emotions No One Else Could See.

You are not broken beyond repair.
You are not your worst moment.
You are worthy of healing and you don't have to do it alone.

Reflection Prompt: Pretty, Perfect, and Falling Apart

- What masks do you wear to feel safe or accepted?
- When was the last time you looked "fine" but were falling apart inside?
- What would it feel like to let people see the real you?

Chapter 4: What They Don'T Tell You About Healing

Always Healing

> *Healing Isn't A Destination, It's A Constant, Uncomfortable, Courageous Process. This Chapter Gives Readers Permission To Take Breaks, To Spiral And Come Back, To Be In Progress Without Shame. It's An Invitation To Keep Showing Up, Even When The Path Doesn't Feel Linear.*

What they don't tell you about healing is that you are always healing. It is in all aspects of your life. I am most comfortable within my bubble of two friends, my dad, and my boys. I am myself, I can say my crazy or do my crazy and I am still loved unconditionally.

Add on a little major depression and anxiety and boom, we have a storm. Anxiety for me is that same fight I grew up doing. I started getting panic attacks as an adult and felt high anxiety in my chest during times I least expected it. That was new for me. It's like my body would turn against me even when I was trying my best to keep things at bay.

It's because I get tired of exhausting my circle. When I'm on my highs and lows, are they. When people deeply care about you, they share your pain and your glory.

You must also know your circle. Sometimes, they love to ride the high with you but not your low. And that hurts, especially when you're the one holding it down during their storms.

You are always healing, even when you don't know you're spiraling. And sometimes you still spiral. What matters is that you keep showing up. Apologize when needed. Take a break from it all if you have to. You will be too much for some, and that's okay. You may have conflicts at work. You may lose friends. Just communicate, advocate, and remove those who don't wish you well or who are triggers for you.

I have to watch people with avoidant personalities. The more they pull away, the more I want to hold on. Even when I know, logically, that person shouldn't even be in my life.

I'm still working on how to handle people who hurt me. Especially in romantic relationships. When you have abandonment issues, sometimes even when you're the one who initiated the goodbye, the need to reattach is strong. Even if the thing is broken. Even if it hurts you. The anger can get extreme. I can love and hate a person within seconds.

BPD Insight: *When Healing Feels Like a Loop*

The truth? Sometimes I get it right. Sometimes I don't.
I still confuse impulse with intuition. I still send the text I swore I wouldn't. I still spiral and then have to self-soothe my way back to center. And sometimes, I *really* need that medicine.

But I'm not ashamed of how hard I work to stay aware, even when it's exhausting. I'm proud of how I reflect instead of react. Healing isn't pretty. It's repetition. It's self-talk. It's trying again.

▶ If you're still learning how to live with it and deal; me too. You're not broken. You're practicing.

Anger is a healthy and realistic emotion. But it's important to use the **right** emotion, not just the most familiar one. Anger is easy for me. It was the first emotion I learned. And I aced it.

But there is also devastation, sadness, hope, opportunity **and healing emotions** that I now allow myself to feel. Sometimes I feel "blah" for no reason at all. And now? I allow that too.

I let myself feel. But I don't wallow.
I give myself a day. And then, no matter what, I get up and try again. Even when I don't want to.

And here's what they *really* don't tell you about healing...

You cannot technically be healed. You are always **healing** because there is no cure for this shit. It is treatable. It is manageable. But it never truly goes away.

Think about it: I knew something was off with me as a little girl. It took 36 years to even begin peeling back the layers. That's my entire adolescent and adult life doing things that weren't healthy.

It's more than just coping; it's doing the work. Over and over again. And if I'm going to be exhausted, I'd rather be exhausted from healing than exhausted because BPD is winning.

They don't tell you that people are afraid of what they don't understand.
They don't tell you that while others judge you already know your demons.
And that's power.

If you're walking around thinking you're totally sane and nothing's wrong with you, I'm scared of *you*.
There is **power** in knowing your weaknesses and using your strengths to improve.

They don't tell you to be proud of yourself.
They don't tell you to celebrate your growth.
But I'm telling you: Be proud.

I haven't cut in years. That doesn't mean I'm no longer a cutter. It means I use the tools I've learned to stay ahead of my breaking point.

Because healing isn't a finish line.
It's a **lifelong commitment to yourself.**
And baby, I'm committed.

Reflection Prompt:

What They Don't Tell You About Healing

- What parts of healing have surprised or disappointed you?
- What toxic truths have you had to unlearn?
- Are you being patient with your own progress?

Chapter 5: Boundaries Saved My Life

'No' is a Full Sentence

> *Boundaries Aren't Just About Saying No, They're About Choosing Peace, Sanity, And Survival. This Chapter Gives Voice To The Messy Power Of Creating Limits, Especially When The World (Or Your Mind) Is Trying To Pull You In Every Direction.*

Creating boundaries is important. It is life-saving.
Boundaries protect your peace, your healing, and your mind. They remind you that you are not required to be everything for everybody, not even for the people who expect it from you.

Understanding your triggers is part of survival. Knowing what and who can set you off, and giving yourself permission to pause or walk away, is one of the bravest things you can do especially when you live with something like BPD.

I had to learn to be patient with myself and others. Because even when you apologize, I guarantee you'll apologize for the same thing more than once. It's not because you're not trying. Sometimes, you just can't see it in the moment. But a boundary? A real one? That's a safe haven. A place where you get to be your full self while also advocating for your needs.

Real Talk: Even Family Can Be a Trigger

I don't come around as much anymore. And I don't feel bad about it. Even family members can be triggers, and you have to learn to love them from a distance.

Just because I'm doing the work, just because I'm self-aware and unpacking my trauma, doesn't mean they are. That's the hardest part.

You start healing and thinking the people closest to you will meet you there but they won't.

I remember one family session that changed my life. It also almost broke me. I poured myself out. Six to ten family members sitting in that room, hearing everything I'd carried. And then... most of them went right back to their lives.
They heard me. But they didn't adhere.
And that hurts in a way that no therapist can fix.

That's the moment I realized: only people willing to do the work with me can stay by my side. And that goes both ways. I'm not perfect. I've triggered people too. But I'm trying. I'm showing up.
And I need people around me who do the same.

The Cousin Who Saw It All

When I was really falling apart, when I was at one of the darkest, most dangerous points in my life, there was one person in my family who showed up in a way I'll never forget: my cousin.

We're six years apart, but pain doesn't care about age. Her presence during that time created my very first true safe space.

She's the one who took me to my very first psychiatric evaluation. The same appointment where they told me I needed inpatient care. I didn't go, because of my boys but she was right there beside me the whole time.

I didn't ask her to step out of the room. I let her stay while I answered every question. Told the whole truth. She was the only person in my family, at the time, I trusted to know just how bad it really was.

She heard about the cutting. The spiraling. The things even my daddy and brother knew but couldn't really speak on.
And it broke her.

She cried right there in the chair beside me.
Because she didn't know.
Because it hurt.
Because some of my pain looked and sounded a little too familiar.

Afterward, she told me she couldn't go to another appointment with me. And she said it with love.

She didn't ghost me. She didn't pretend.
She communicated it clearly.
She said, "I love you, but I have to protect my own peace."

And I respected that. I *loved* her for that. Because that's what real love looks like. It's honest. It's boundary-honoring. It doesn't require sacrifice to be sincere.

From then on, she'd check in on me in her own way. Dropping little nuggets about her own mental health journey so I wouldn't feel alone. Just enough to remind me: *you still got me.*

She holds a permanent place in my heart for that. When I think back to the first time I admitted how far gone I was, she was sitting right beside me. And I'll never forget it.

Some people won't respect that you're sick.
Some will agitate, antagonize, and gaslight you on purpose, knowing full well what you're battling. Whether it's a personality trait or intentional cruelty, it's dangerous. Because that's when BPD whispers:

"See? I told you they didn't love you."
"They didn't check on you. Didn't call. Didn't even care when you were in therapy."

Those moments give the disorder a microphone.
And if you're not careful, you'll believe it again.

🧠 BPD Insight: *Boundaries as Armor*

BPD will convince you that you're too much—
Too emotional. Too unstable. Too hard to love.

But boundaries are how I push back.

I can be loved and still have limits.
I can need space and still be worthy.
I can forgive you and still walk away.

I'm not cold. I'm not cruel. I'm protecting my peace.

▶ Boundaries saved my life and they keep saving it every time I say *no to chaos*, *yes to peace*, and *choose myself*, again and again.

The Diagnosis That Shook Me

Hearing the diagnosis was both devastating and relieving.
Finally, a name for what had been plaguing me for decades.

But then came the bigger question:
Now that I know… how do I fix it?
How do I live with it?

You cannot do it alone. You just can't.
You need clinical help.
You need support.
You need tools.

If it weren't for medication, breathing techniques, journal writing, extensive therapy, I don't know where I'd be. Honestly? Probably dead.

A statistic. Another Black woman who lost her battle to suicide while the world whispered about how "selfish" she was.

And you know what they would forget?

They would forget all the good.
All the love I gave.
All the lives I touched.
All the laughter, the lessons, the loyalty.

Because when someone dies by suicide, people forget everything else and call you weak.
But the truth is: I was fighting a battle every single day.
And I'm still fighting.

I'm better now.
I'm healing.
I'm trying.
And I'll keep trying for the rest of my life.

Yes, I still get scared. I'm afraid of pushing people away. Afraid that I'll end up alone because I ran everyone off. That's how BPD talks to you. That's the poison it pours in your ears when things get quiet.

That's why I stay in the work.
That's why I show up.
That's why I share my story.

Because someone out there is just like me and she needs to know that she is not alone.

I've started exploring more healing practices:

- Books and memoirs from women like me.
- EMDR (Eye Movement Desensitization and Reprocessing).
- DBT (Dialectical Behavioral Therapy).
- Support groups and soul circles.

Because the more I heal myself, the more I can help break generational curses.

My sons are watching.

And I refuse to pass down what nearly destroyed me.

Reflection Prompt: *Boundaries Saved My Life*

- Where are you still saying yes when your soul is screaming no?
- Who taught you that boundaries were selfish?
- What's one small boundary you can set this week?

Chapter 6: I Am Not My Diagnosis

Fighting the BPD Narrative

> *This Chapter Is A Reclamation. A Declaration. You're Not Crazy. You're Not Weak. You're Not Defined By Letters On A Chart. It's A Bold Pushback Against Stigma And A Reminder That Healing Is Possible, Even When The Diagnosis Tries To Speak Louder Than Your Truth.*

It's been about ten years since I first heard the words: Borderline Personality Disorder. A decade of learning to manage a mind that sometimes feels like a war zone. About a year ago, I went back to therapy and really reflected on the journey. And let me tell you— knowing what to do doesn't mean it's always easy to do it.

I've learned strategies. I know how to soothe myself, rubbing my thighs to ground myself, holding a sentimental trinket, praying, fasting, breathing. I've learned to sit in it, even when it feels unbearable. That's the part most people avoid, sitting in the darkness. It's loud, haunting, and real. But avoiding it only lets it fester. You can't heal what you're constantly running from.

The hardest part of BPD? Feeling like I'm always too much to be loved. I don't mean "kind of difficult", I mean fully believing that no matter how kind, successful, funny, or giving I am, I'll always be one meltdown away from being "too much." That fear shows up heavy in relationships.

When someone asks me what I want in a partner, I say: *"To feel safe."* And I don't mean financially, I mean emotionally. I want to know that even when I'm spiraling or shutting down, you won't leave. That kind of trust takes years, and most people I meet haven't had the time to build it. My friends? They've been around 20+ years. They know my silences. They know when I need tough love or just grace.

But a new man? He don't know all that. And BPD whispers: *"It's your fault."* When it might not be. It might be his unhealed trauma. It might be timing. But I'm always holding the weight of being "the problem."

And then there's society: telling little girls since birth that Barbie needs a Ken. That something's wrong with you if you're not boo'd up. I could have everything; house, career, bomb-ass kids and still feel not enough because I don't have a partner. That's BPD, too.

You learn to be careful with your story. Not everyone deserves the full version. I've done things I'm not proud of at jobs, in relationships, with friends. I've used fists when I should've used words. I've made impulsive decisions. But I'm still here. Still working. Still healing.

Mental illness is like any other illness. It affects your life, but it doesn't define it. People think it's shameful, but it's not. You wouldn't shame someone for diabetes or sickle cell. Why do it with BPD?

Still, I've learned to discern. Not everyone gets access to my past. Not everyone deserves to hear about the scars, the breakdowns, the hospital stays. Some things are for me, my therapist, and maybe a trusted few. Because not everyone has the depth or compassion to hold that kind of truth. And that's okay.

 BPD Insight: *We Bend; We Don't Break*

People with BPD are not broken.
We are wired to feel deeply, respond intensely, and love hard.

That intensity isn't a flaw; it's a feature.
But even passion needs practice.

We still need tools.
We still need support.
We still need space to grow.

**▶ You're not too much, you're just still becoming.
And no matter how far you bend, you *don't break*.**

I no longer get offended when someone I trust says, "Did you take your medicine?" Because sometimes, I do need to take that medicine. I need my journal. My walks. My sweatpants and silence. And I need my three positives for every one negative.

Anger was my first language, but now I speak more than rage. I speak truth. I speak calm. I speak softness, even when it feels foreign.

I see myself in my sons. Oooh, they got that little-man syndrome and them tempers. Even my dog got an attitude. But we're learning—together. I'm teaching them to breathe through it, to talk through it. And therapy didn't just save me; it's helping them, too.

After ten years of living with BPD, I've learned to ask better questions. I want to know your attachment style, your conflict resolution skills, your love language. I don't want to fall in love with a trigger. I want peace. I want consistency. I want love without chaos.

I've also learned this hard truth: you can tell someone your whole story, scream your needs, and still be left. Some people only come for your energy, your beauty, or your body. They don't have the capacity to be your soft place. And when that happens, you gotta walk away healthy, without the breakdown. Without the spiral.

That's growth.

You are not your diagnosis.
You are not your past.
You are not "too much."
You are someone who's learning to feel, love, and survive with softness.

And that? That's powerful.

Reflection Prompt:

I Am Not My Diagnosis

- What labels have you carried that don't define you?
- How does stigma affect how you view yourself?
- What would self-compassion sound like if it had your voice?

Chapter 7: Healing Is Not Linear

It Aint No Straight Line, Sis

> *This Chapter Is A Truth Bomb. Healing Is Messy, Non-Linear, And Often Unfair. It's The Two-Steps-Forward, Five-Steps-Back Dance That No One Prepares You For. But Every Time You Get Back Up—That's Progress.*

What they don't tell you about healing is this: you are always healing. **Always.**

There is no finish line. No big "aha" moment where you finally become whole and stay that way forever. Healing don't come with a checklist, and it sure as hell don't come in a straight line.

Healing is a lifetime process that touches every part of your world, your relationships, your parenting, your job, your habits, and especially that unfiltered voice in your own head. It's layered. And exhausting. And sacred.

I'm most at peace inside my bubble. My boys. My two closest friends. My daddy. That's my sanctuary. Those are the people who see me, mess and all and still choose to love me through it. With them, I can exhale. I can be Nikki. I can say my crazy, do my crazy, and still be wrapped in grace.

But real healing? It don't just happen in soft spaces.
It shows up in the hard moments. The unexpected ones.

Throw in BPD, anxiety, and major depression, and baby, sometimes I feel like I'm weathering a storm with no umbrella.
For me, anxiety feels like every fight I've ever had to survive growing up. It sits heavy in my chest. It creeps up on calm days, reminding me that my nervous system still thinks I'm in danger, even when I'm safe.

 **BPD Insight:** *The Loop is Real*

With BPD, emotions don't just visit, they take over.
You can go from laughing to crying to rage… all in one conversation.

And then?
You replay the whole scene in your mind a hundred times.
That's the loop.

Was I overreacting?
Did I say too much?
Am I too much?

That emotional whiplash is real.
It makes healing harder because sometimes, you don't know if what you're feeling is real… or just loud.

▶ **But being aware of the loop is the first step to stepping out of it.**
Awareness is power. And you've already started.

Panic attacks hit me in adulthood, and they don't play fair.
They show up when I'm trying to be strong. When I'm minding my business. When I'm trying my best. It's like my body remembers battles I thought I already won.

And then comes the guilt. Because when I crash, my people feel it too. I don't want to drain them. When I'm soaring, they celebrate with me. But when I sink, they go down too. That's love. But it's also heavy.

So I get quiet. I isolate. Not because I'm mad at anyone, but because I don't want to break the people I love while I'm trying to fix myself.

But here's the hard truth: not everyone in your life can hold space for your healing.
Some will cheer when you're glowing, but disappear when you're

unraveling.

Some will love you conditionally, when you're "easy to love," when you're not asking too much.

That's why your circle matters.

You gotta know who's really riding with you.

I've had to learn the difference between support and proximity. Between people who are present, and people who are actually present for you.

Sometimes you have to step back, not out of spite, but out of survival. Because protecting your peace isn't selfish. It's sacred.

And baby, healing is sacred.

It's not always pretty. Sometimes it looks like ugly crying behind the wheel. Sometimes it's canceling everything on your calendar because you can't fake one more smile. Sometimes it's disappearing for a day or a week, just to feel like you again.

But even when I break, I show up.
Even when I spiral, I return.
Even when I fall apart, I pick up the pieces.

That's the healing.
That's the work.
And no, it ain't no straight line, sis. But it's still forward.

Reflection Prompt:

The Sacred Work of Healing

• What does healing look like for you right now—in this season of your life?
• Who are the people in your life that make you feel safe to unravel and rebuild?
• Where in your life are you still pretending to be okay just to keep others comfortable?
• What would it feel like to protect your peace without guilt?

Chapter 8: Keeping Your Shit Together

Because Falling Apart Ain't Always an Option

> *This speaks to the raw truth: holding it down at work, at home, and for your boys, even when you feel like unraveling. It's the real-life survival mode you know too well, especially in leadership roles.*

I'm still learning how to read the room, how to show up as Ms. Alleyne at work and switch back to Nikki when I'm off. I've got to keep my free-spirited self in check, so I don't say the wrong thing, give too much, or lose my cool over something small… especially when what triggered me wasn't even work-related.

That's the thing about BPD: when your personal life is crumbling and your emotions are slipping through your fingers, you still have to show up. You still have to be somebody's mama, somebody's boss, somebody's everything. You can't always take a mental health day, especially not in my line of work.

Some days, I'm just trying to make it to the end of the day so I can go home and sit in silence. Sit in my "nothing box." Just exist. Just breathe. Just be.

But even that gets exhausting. Sometimes I look at myself like, *Damn, why can't I get it together?*

I was angry when I first got diagnosed. Mad as hell. All that childhood trauma built me into a woman who now has what, *a personality disorder?* It felt like my inner pain had finally caught up to me and dragged a label behind it. That shit might be cute if you're Beyoncé and can rename yourself Sasha Fierce, but for me? It felt heavy, shameful, lonely.

I used to blame it on not having a mother. Or maybe if my dad had gotten me into therapy earlier. He tried once, in seventh grade, with some older white woman who didn't ask the right questions and couldn't connect with me. I went five years in adult therapy before I ever admitted I still cut when I was upset. Five. Years.

Anxiety and major depression? Sure, I'd heard of those. But BPD? That wasn't talked about where I'm from. Especially not in the Black community. We weren't raised to believe in mental health, let alone something so stigmatized. I had to research it myself. Had to figure out what it meant to live with it, and if that meant I was broken beyond repair.

And there wasn't much out there, at least not enough of *our* stories. Not from high-functioning Black women like me who manage to lead, raise kids, and hold shit down… even while falling apart inside.

Am I really high-functioning? Or am I just polished at packaging the chaos?

Sometimes I wonder: Can I actually help someone else? Will they even listen or will they just judge?

That isolation is what hurts the most. The fear that people, friends, jobs, men; will run when they hear the truth. That once you name it, they'll Google it… and disappear.

I get the same feedback often. "You're too much." "You can do more." When I start a new job, I try to be quiet at first, trying not to overwhelm folks. But coworkers are not as forgiving as friends. Especially when you work in a high-performing culture where mental health days don't exist, and your job is literally to *take care of others*.

 **BPD Insight:** *The Invisible Load*

People think BPD only shows up in toxic relationships, but it follows you to work, too.

It's the overthinking after a meeting.
The spiraling after feedback.
The pressure to be perfect, liked, and in control... even when you're falling apart inside.

High-functioning folks with BPD get praised for being strong, passionate, and "on it."
But they don't see the crash that comes later.
The meltdown in the car.
The emotional hangover.
The fear that one wrong move could cost you *everything*.

▶ That's the invisible load.
And we carry it, while still showing up, still smiling, still surviving.

That's part of why I ended up in special education. Ironically, what I have wouldn't have even qualified me for school accommodations under the law but I sure need some now. As an adult, I have to create my own "accommodations." I carve out quiet time in the morning before the world starts. I sit in my car, my garage, wherever I can find peace.

Because no matter what, people are counting on me.

I don't have the luxury of losing my shit in public. I can't afford to blow up at work. I don't always get to fall apart.

So, I keep my personal issues personal. Not every workplace is safe. Not everyone will understand. But even if I'm unraveling inside, I show up. I do the job. I take care of the kids. I keep the house running. Because falling apart just ain't always an option.

Reflection Prompt: Keeping Your Shit Together

- What parts of your life look "together" but feel fragile behind the scenes?

- What's the cost of high-functioning survival?

- What would it mean to keep it together *without* losing yourself?

Chapter 9: How To Love Me (And People Like Me)

A Soft Guide for the Ones Who Choose Stay

> *This Reflection Softens The Edge Of The Chapter And Centers Both Accountability And Compassion. It Lets The Reader And The People Who Love You Know That You're Not Asking For Perfection. You're Just Asking For Effort And Understanding. You Don't Want To Be Fixed. You Want To Be Met.*

I've talked a lot in this book about surviving me.
But the truth is, there are people who choose to love me, stay with me, and grow with me, even when it's not easy.
They deserve space in this story too.

People who love me almost always come back.
Sometimes, they just need a break from me and now, I'm finally okay with that.

That used to make me spiral.
I called it abandonment, assumed the worst, and punished myself (or them) for the space.

Now I recognize it for what it is: **space.**
And I've grown enough to know that I can be a lot.

Not bad. Not broken. Just… **intense.**

That intensity used to scare people off.
Now? The right people simply adjust the volume when they need to breathe.

Real-Life Examples:

My best guy friend in New York is a true introvert who loves me unconditionally.

He knows my patterns. He knows my heart. And he knows I talk a mile a minute when I'm emotionally lit up.
So sometimes, he'll look at me and say:
"Hey Notorious (his perfect nickname for me), I need a minute. Shush."
And I don't take it personally.
Because I know he means it with love.

That's not rejection, it's **rhythm.**
That's what boundaries look like in real relationships.

Then there's my best friend and sister, an extroverted introvert with a slick mouth and a deep soul.
She'll tell me when I've crossed a line, when she needs a break, or when I'm spiraling a little too loud.
And even when her delivery has a little sting on it, I know her intention is love.
She's not trying to hurt me, she's trying to stay connected without losing herself.

That kind of honesty used to terrify me.
Now I crave it.
Because I want to know when I'm being too much, not so I can shrink, but so I can love people well, too.

A Word from a Friend

Sometimes, the people who love me see things I can't.
This is how one of my closest friends described what it's like to support me during a spiral.
They didn't say it to be poetic. They said it to help me understand myself.

"When you are spiraling, I know you don't need advice…"

At first, I didn't get it.
But what they said next hit me in my chest:

When I'm spiraling, logic doesn't land.
Suggestions feel like pressure.
And attention, even when it's nurturing, can unintentionally feed the spiral.
Because BPD sometimes clings to what it didn't get enough of: affection, attention, comfort.

But space?
Space helps me sort through the noise.
It helps me separate what's real from what I *feel*.

That's what real love looks like sometimes, **loving distance**.
Not abandonment. Not silence.
Just enough room for me to find my footing without losing their presence.

And in those moments, that's the greatest kind of love.

 BPD Insight: *How to Love Us*

Loving someone with BPD doesn't mean walking on eggshells.
It means learning the rhythm of their nervous system, their needs, their fears.
And finding your own boundaries within that love.

You don't have to save them.
Just see them.
Hear them.
Stay honest.

Be willing to learn their language of love.
Because love doesn't have to be loud.

▶ But it *does* need to be real.

Reflective Pause:

Think about a time when you needed space but didn't know how to ask for it.
Now think about someone in your life who may have needed space from you.

- How did you respond?
- Did it feel like rejection or did you recognize it as a form of love?
- If you're loving someone with BPD, what are some ways you can show up without losing yourself?
- If you are someone with BPD, what are some ways you can communicate your needs without guilt or fear?

Try writing a letter (just for you) that starts with:
"Here's how I need to be loved and here's how I promise to love better too."

This is how we make space for healing.
This is how we love each other better.
And this is how we stay.

Reflection Prompt: How to Love Me (and People Like Me)

• Who are the people in your life that know how to love you well—and what makes their love feel safe?
• When have you needed space in a relationship but didn't know how to ask for it?
• How can you better communicate your needs without guilt and respect others' boundaries without fear?

Chapter 10: When The Rage Took Over

A Record of Wreckage, and the Grace That Saved Me

> *This Chapter Isn't Just A List Of Wild Moments Or Broken Relationships, It's Me Holding The Mirror Up To The Harm I've Caused While Living With Borderline Personality Disorder. The Rage Wasn't Always Justified, But It Was Real. This Is A Record Of The Wreckage, Yes, But It's Also A Testimony To The Grace That Found Me In The Middle Of It. The Love I Didn't Think I Deserved. The Growth I Didn't Think Was Possible. This Is Where Survival Meets Accountability.*

The rage didn't start in adulthood. It had roots in my childhood, where I sometimes responded to emotional pain by trying to control my environment in unhealthy ways. I didn't understand the difference between power and pain. What looked like "acting out" was actually a deep, unspoken struggle to make sense of my world and protect myself from it.

My mind stayed busy, and the second I got hurt or ignored, I'd go from zero to fire.

You gotta be careful what you feed into your brain too. Those crime shows and murder docs? Baby, that stuff is dangerous when you already got BPD whispering in your ear, taking notes in the background.

And don't let me be sipping or something, that's gasoline on a flame.
I check off every damn box on the list for this diagnosis.
Add trauma, abandonment, and being highly educated and socially charming?
That's a ticking time bomb with a degree and a cute smile.

Black-and-white thinking is one of the worst parts of BPD.
You're either with me or against me.
There's no in-between.

One minute I'm riding for you like nobody else. The next, you're dead to me.
And I might try to resurrect you the next day like nothing happened.
That switch? It's terrifying.

There were times in my life when emotional pain pushed me past my limits. I lashed out, said things I regretted, and reacted in ways that caused harm to others and to myself. I'm not proud of those moments, but I don't hide from them either. I share them not to glorify the chaos, but to show how untreated trauma can explode into actions that don't align with who you really are. Healing helped me close that gap.

Sometimes I didn't even know why I was so mad, just that they messed up.
And the truth?
Half the time, they didn't even know they were being ranked so high in my world.

That's the danger of BPD: we glorify people silently.
We put them in sacred places in our hearts; friends, lovers, co-workers, expecting loyalty, perfection, consistency.
And when they fall short of that invisible standard?
The fall is hard.
The rage ain't just about what they did, it's about what I built them up to be.

That's the heartbreak.
That's the betrayal.
That's the root.

I've done things I regret, things I never imagined someone like me would do. Some moments are seared into my memory because they marked rock bottom. But here's the truth: I was hurting. I didn't have the language or the tools. My reactions weren't about causing harm, they were about escaping it. With therapy, self-awareness, and support, I no longer lead with reactivity. I lead with reflection.

The one I spiraled on in that bar?
He wasn't just some guy; I adored him.
And the one I broke down on in that little club?
We had six years of history. He never raised his voice at me.
None of them ever did.
But back then, I wasn't in control of my rage, I was surviving it.

But that didn't stop me.

I don't always feel guilty about what I've done.
But I do feel something.
Shame.
Frustration.
Embarrassment; for losing my cool in public.
Back then, I didn't know how to pause.
Didn't know how to pull myself out of the spiral before it swallowed me.
And though I can't undo those moments, I've done the work to understand them.
I've done the work to make sure they don't define me. Because I know better.

I've got the degrees. The accolades. The leadership roles.
I'm doing the damn thing in real life.
So why am I out here ready to wreck it all behind somebody without vision and definitely no business being in my circle to begin with?

That's the part that eats me up.

That I've done enough work to know better, and still, sometimes, I slide.
I spiral.
And then I beat myself up even harder after.
Because I know better.

That's why emotional regulation is so damn important.
You can't ride the highs and lows and think it won't cost you something.
You have to find your steady level and stay there.

When you feel that toxic energy creeping in, when a man is showing you he's not right, when a woman is poking at your peace, when your BPD starts whispering, you gotta choose something else.

Go walk.
Call your girlfriends.
Do a stretch.
Join a free fitness session.
Watch a movie.
Call your damn therapist.

Do anything but let the disorder amp you up into losing everything you've worked for.

Because it's not just about avoiding conflict.
It's about protecting your progress.

Setting boundaries.
Practicing coping tools.
Making healthy decisions about who gets access to you.

Nobody belongs on a pedestal.
That's not love. That's a setup.

🧠 BPD Insight: *When Rage is Survival*

Borderline rage isn't just anger.
It's survival mode.

It's your body reacting to emotional injury like it's life or death,
Because for someone with BPD, that's how abandonment feels.
That's how betrayal feels.

The reaction might not be rational.
But the pain behind it is real.

▶ Don't dismiss the rage.
Understand the wound beneath it.

I once chased a person through my neighborhood in my daddy F150 truck like it was a damn movie scene.

I used to go from explosive to unfazed in minutes.
There were moments; too many, where I snapped without warning...
and then sat down like nothing happened.
No aftermath. No apology.
Just me, ordering wings while everyone else tried to catch their breath.
That's the part people never saw coming.
Not the rage, but the silence after. That's the cycle:
rage → release → reset.

And the people who love me?
They know.
They know when to give space.
When to shut up.
When not to try and fix it because trying to reason with me mid-spiral only makes it worse.

Even nurturing too much can prolong the episode, because BPD feeds off attention and affection, the very things I didn't get when I needed them most.

And yet, the quiet?
That pause?
That step-back?

That's sometimes the only thing that grounds me and helps me see facts over feelings.
Because in the moment, I will convince myself your suggestion won't work,
that the world is ending,
and that you are the enemy.

Then two hours later, I might be laughing and fine again, like none of it happened.
That's the whiplash of emotional dysregulation.

This isn't to excuse what I've done.
It's to name it.
To own it.
To check myself.
To remind myself that growth means choosing something different *before* the spiral; not just apologizing after it.

I still struggle sometimes.
But I'm not who I was.
And I'm not going back.

BPD Insight: *Silence Can Be Support*

People with BPD don't always need to be comforted in the storm.
They need space to *see* the storm.

Sometimes silence, when offered with love,
Is more grounding than words.

Because logic doesn't land mid-spiral.
It only enters *after* the fire dies down.

▶ Give us room to return to ourselves.
That's where the healing starts.

Reflection Prompt: *Survival Mode Isn't Love*

- Have you ever been the hurricane? Not the victim, but the storm?
- What relationships didn't survive your reaction?
- What would accountability, not shame, look like for you now?
- Who did you place on a pedestal, and what did it cost you?
- What's your go-to strategy when you feel yourself slipping into chaos?

Final Chapter: The Girl Outside The Door

I'm Still Guarding My Peace

This Ties Beautifully Back To The Image Of Little Nikki Sitting Outside Her Daddy's Door. It's Powerful. It Speaks To Protection, Vulnerability, Growth, And Full-Circle Healing. A Grown Woman Still Standing Watch But This Time, Over Herself.

I remember asking my daddy to tell me stories, because some parts of my childhood are blurry. But this one stuck. He told me that when I was little, I would sit outside his bedroom door and not move. With my toys, quietly waiting. Guarding it. He knew I was serious about that door. I didn't want him to leave. I didn't want anyone else to leave me again.

My mama didn't leave me when I was five weeks old. She started abusing drugs then. I don't remember exactly when she physically left, but I was old enough to know she wasn't coming back. Maybe around three. Old enough for it to hurt. Old enough to remember the absence. The disappointment. That kind of wound doesn't heal easily, it lingers, sits in your chest, and whispers to you in quiet moments. It tells you people you love will always leave.

So I clung to my daddy. He was my safe place. Still is. My best friend, but still my father. He's the man I used to fear. The one whose voice could make me jump. The man who raised me with discipline and structure, who didn't allow crying or softness, who told me to "just get some Jesus" and keep going. We didn't always speak the same emotional language, but he tried. And he's still trying. I will always be grateful for him.

That little girl sitting outside the door never left me. She shows up when I'm scared, when I feel abandoned, when I'm triggered. But now,

I see her differently. She was never weak, she was holding the line. She was protecting the last piece of stability she had. That girl was strong.

🧠 BPD Insight: *Healing the Inner Child*

Borderline Personality Disorder often roots itself in childhood trauma.
In broken bonds. In unmet needs. In a fragile sense of self.

That's why the fear of abandonment cuts so deep.
Why identity feels like it's always shifting.

But healing doesn't mean forgetting.
It doesn't mean erasing the past.

▶ It means learning how to hold space for the child you were.
While creating safety for the adult you've become.

Today, I'm still that girl. But now I guard myself. I guard my peace. I protect my space, my heart, my healing. I make different choices now. I show up for myself. And when I don't feel like I can? I rest, but I don't quit.

My life is worth fighting for.

My son, the one who doesn't even believe in all this mental health stuff, once said, *"Mom, one day we'll have kids. You gotta be here for your grandkids. Think about how far you'll move up in education in another 10 years. Think about watching us thrive. You gotta be here for that."*

And he's right. I've got more life to live. I've got healing to do. I've got joy to experience. I've got people to love and people who love me.

I may not always know the way forward, but I will always guard the door. And this time, it's the door to me.

♥ FINAL REFLECTION – THE LAST WORD

Final Reflection:

I'm still her. That little girl. Sitting on the floor, outside her daddy's door, hoping someone would open up and see her. But I've also become the woman who holds her hand now.

This book is not a declaration of arrival. It's a record of survival. It's the messy middle, the sacred in-between, the part of the story most people skip over or hide. But I don't want to hide anymore.

If you made it to the end of this book, I pray you see your own strength more clearly. I hope you know now that trauma doesn't get the last word, *you do*. And healing? It doesn't have to be perfect to be real.

Keep guarding your peace. Keep choosing yourself. And when the world gets too loud, remember:
You don't have to explain your pain to anyone to be worthy of healing.

About the Author

N. Alleyne is an educator, advocate, and storyteller known for her work in special education, school leadership, and mental health awareness. A proud native of Houston's Fifth Ward, Nikki has built a career on speaking truth to power, whether in boardrooms, classrooms, or between the pages of her first book.

Diagnosed with Borderline Personality Disorder after years of being misunderstood, Nikki turned her healing journey into a lifeline for others. Her writing blends raw honesty, southern humor, and deep insight to shed light on the complexity of living with BPD as a high-functioning Black woman.

When she's not working as an Assistant Principal or building her advocacy company, *Angie Cares,* Nikki can be found blasting old school R&B, spoiling her emotional support dog Lorenzo, or laughing too loud with her sons, Kamryn and Kaeden. She is a firm believer in boundaries, Black girl joy, and breaking generational curses, one honest conversation at a time.

Follow her journey at:
- Instagram: @ac_parentadvocacy
- Email: nicolette.alleyne@yahoo.com

About the Book

This is not a memoir built for sympathy.
This is a truth-telling, gut-spilling, healing-wrapped-in-honesty kind of book, for anyone who's ever had to survive their own mind and still show up to work the next day.

With raw vulnerability, Alleyne cracks open the stigma of BPD and reveals the whole picture: the rage, the softness, the shame, the joy, the breakdowns, and the bounce-backs.

Through powerful storytelling, personal reflections, BPD insights, and deeply emotional moments, she invites you to sit beside her inner child, the girl who guarded her peace even when the world wouldn't protect it.

This book is for:

- People navigating BPD and tired of being misunderstood
- Partners, friends, and family members trying to love someone with big emotions
- Anyone healing childhood wounds while still showing up grown

This isn't a how-to.
It's a "me too."
A mirror for the hurting, the healing, and the ones who want to stay.

www.ingramcontent.com/pod-product-compliance
Lightning Source LLC
Chambersburg PA
CBHW020218090426
42734CB00008B/1115